한·영 시선집
감잎 단풍에 담은 연서

시인의 마을 시선집 35

# 청학 정삼일 한 · 영 시선집
# 감잎 단풍에 담은 연서

황금동산(무학산)에 있는 시비

**도서출판 한글**

20대 때의 문학소년

언제

어느 때 만나도

반가운 사람이 되었으면

좋겠습니다.

_____님에게

한·영 시선집을 드립니다.

년    월    일

# 한·영 시선집을 내면서

 비가 좋아서, 비 오는 날이면 우산을 들고 비 맞으면서 무작정 걷다가 통행금지 시간이 되면 여관에서 머물다 통행금지 끝나는 새벽에 집에 들어와서 곤한 잠을 자듯이, 소년 시절에 외로움과 방황하던 시절 시를 쓰지 않으면 안 되었기에 쓰기 시작한 지가 엊그제 같은데 50여 년이 흘렀으니 세월이 참 빠른 것을 느끼며, 후회하지 않고 시인으로 부끄러운 삶을 살지 않으려고 노력하며 살아왔습니다.

주간 「한국문학신문」 '영역시 감상하기' 2015년 12월 9일 제236호 '행복을 위하여'부터 2019년 12월 18일 제430호 '병풍'까지 만 4년 동안(제1시집부터 제5시집 중에서 선별한 시 75편을 번역하여) 연재한 시를 한·영 시선집으로 출간하게 되었습니다.

한·영 시선집 출간에 주간 「한국문학신문」 '영역시 감상하기'에 실어주신 임수홍 사장님, 번역을 해주신 김연복 선생님(11편), 진철보 선생님(64편)과 출판을 맡아주신 도서출판 한글 심혁창(아동문학가) 사장님에게 고마움을 전합니다. 이제는 언제, 어느 때 만나더라도 반가운 사람이면 좋겠습니다.

2023년 황금동 무학산에서

靑鶴 鄭 三 一

# Publishing Korean-English Anthology

I like rain. When I was young, I used to walk in the rain aimlessly without knowing the time flowing and stopped by the midnight curfew. Then I stayed at a nearby inn, returned home next morning and fell in sound sleep again. I began to write the lonesome of my young days in poems 50 years ago, but I feel as if such things happened just yesterday. Truly the time flies like an arrow. I wonder if I have tried to live as a right poet so far.

The Weekly Korean Literature Newspaper has published the column of English-translated Poem Appreciation」. They published issue number 236 in December 9 of 2015 and continued to issue number 430 in December 18 of 2019. For four years my collection of poems, book 1 through book 5, were appeared in the papers. I chose 75 poems out of them to be published.

I would like to express my appreciation to The Weekly Korean Literature Newspaper Director Im Su-hong who published serially my poems in 'English-translated Poem Appreciation', to Mr. Kim Yeon-bok who translated my poems into English(11), and to another translator Mr. Jin Cheol-bo(64), and Mr. Sim Hyuk-chang(writer of juvenile stories) who is going to publish my poems into a book.

I hope we are the people who are glad to see each other whenever and wherever.

In the year of 2023

Cheonghak Jeong Sam-il

In Mt. Muhak at Hwanggeumdong

# 목   차

제2시집 『고독한 날개』 중에서
Collection of Poems Ⅱ, 『Lonely wings』

---

제3시집 / 『혼자라는 것이 외로운 건 아니다』중에서
Collection of Poems Ⅲ, 『Single is not lonely』

---

제4시집 『황금동 연가』중에서
Collection of Poems Ⅳ,
『Love Poems of Hwanggeumdong』

---

제5시집 『행복을 위하여』중에서
Collection of Poems V, 『For the Sake of Happiness』

---

제1시집 『바람도 깨지 않게』 중에서
Collection of Poems 1,
『Not Even Awaking up Wind』

# 내가 글을 쓰듯이

당신이
오실 줄 알았습니다.
비록, 조그마한 시화전
가난한 마음에
가난한 시

벌과 나비는
꿀을 찾아 헤매듯이
당신은
연한 얼굴로 이글대며
마음에 양식을 찾아
이글 앞에
오리라고 믿고 있었습니다.

때 묻은 세상
하루를 팔아
하루를 살아가는 인생
당신과 난
남몰래 피었다 지는
꽃일지라도
우리, 서로 사랑하며 삽시다.

# As if I make poems

I knew you would come
To my small illustrated-poem show
Of humble mind
and humble poems

Like bees and butterflies
Fly around to get honey.
I know
You would come
With bright face with smile
To feed your soul
With my writings

In this contaminated world
People sell a day to live a day
Even though yu and I
Are hidden flowers
Blooming and dying in secret
Lets live in love, you and I

Translated by Jin, Cheol-Bo

비록, 적으나마
정성껏
내가 글을 쓰듯이
당신이
내 글을 본다면
서로 사랑했던들
그게 뭐 죄가 됩니까?

Even though
My writings are poor
If you read my poems
After knowing my sincerity
Then, our love each other
Can be a sin?

Translated by Jin, Cheol-Bo

# 자화상(自畵像)

내 어느 뉘 기다림에
鶴이 되었나

물이
흘러가듯이

바위에 닿으면
바위를 빗겨가고

나무에 부딪치면
나무를 빗겨 가듯

물 같은
人生

내 어느 뉘 기다림에
鶴이 되었나

# Self Portrait

Waiting for whom
Have I become a long-necked crane !

My life
Like a stream of water

Avoiding rocks
Or trees

If they are
On my way...

My life like that
Of water...

Looking forward to seeing whom
Have I become a long-necked crane !

Translated by Kim, Yuhn-Bok

# 뉘 까닭이오리까?

그대를 못 잊어
못내 아쉬워함은
뉘 까닭이오리까?

당신 잘못이라면
잃어버리면 되고,

내 잘못이라면
생각 말면 되는데,

그대를 못 잊어
못내 아쉬워함은
뉘 까닭이오리까?

# Because of Who

Because of who
I don't forget
And miss you?

If it were because of you
I can leave you

If it were because of me
I can quit my thinking

Because of who
I can't forget
And miss you?

Translated by Jin, Cheol-Bo

# 바람도 깨지 않게

바람도 깨지 않게
사푼히 사라지세요!
간다고, 간다고는 마세요
아니라고 돌아서 말할지라도
가지 않겠어요!

갈 때도 나 모르게 가세요
미련도, 아쉬움도
안녕! 이란 인사도 남기지 말고
바람도 깨지 않게
사뿐히 사라지세요!

멀리 말고 가까이
바람 불면 옷자락 스칠 곳으로
가든 길도, 되돌아 올 수 있는 곳으로
바람도 깨지 않게
사푼히 사라지세요!

# Not Even Awaking up  Wind

Please fade away
Without awakening a wind
Don't say ″ I will go away ″
Again and again
For I won't go to meet you again
Even though you deny it

Go away without my notice
And without regret or anxiety
Fade away without a farewell
And without awakening a wind

Don't go away too far, stay
Where my clothes can touch you
Come back to me again
Without awakening a wind

Translate by Kim, Yuhn-Bok

# 세월

가누나 가누나…
하나도 가고, 둘도 가고, 셋도…
열둘도 이제는 가려고 하는구나!
무정한 세월은 오늘도 아랑곳없이
흘러흘러 어디론지 가려고 하는구나!
넌, 흘러 흐르러 가면 그만이지만
나의 이마엔 주름살이 느는구나!

가누나 가누나…
하나도 가고, 둘도 가고, 셋도…
열둘도 이제는 가려고 하는구나!
골동품은 날이 가면 갈수록 좋으련만
깊은 산골에 나뭇잎 하나 붙은 나무는
나이테 하나 늘어 감을 슬퍼하며
나의 머리엔 백발이 느는구나!

가누나 가누나…
하나도 가고, 둘도 가고, 셋도…
열둘도 이제는 가려고 하는구나!
너도 가고, 나도 가야 하지만
늙더라도 우리는 젊은 그날같이
넌 나의 소녀, 난 너의 소년이 되어
더욱더 사랑하여 보자꾸나!

# Time

Gone, gone....
One was gone, two was gone, three was gone ....
Now twelve is going away.
Mindless time even today
Is flowing away to somewhere
You are fine by flowing away
But I gets more wrinkles on my forehead.

Gone, gone....
One was gone, two was gone, three was gone ....
Now twelve is going away
Antiques are happy by time passing
But a tree with a last leaf in a deep valley
Is sad by getting another age ring
My head gets more and more white hair

Gone, gone....
One was gone, two was gone, three was gone ....
Now twelve is going away.
You and I have to go
Our bodies get old but our minds stay young
You are my girl and I am your boy
And we do love more and more

Translated by Jin, Cheol-Bo

# 선의 질투

선과 선의 교차점에선
이루지 못하는 선
이것은 선의 질투

아름답던 그 선이
다른 선에 파괴되어
하나의 곡선을 이룬다
이 곡선을 누가 봤는가?

이 아름다움을 보고
질투하기 때문에
선을 두지는 않을 것이다.

- 선이 파괴되면
  곡선이 된다. -

# Jealousy of lines

When a line and a line are being entangled
The lines form a fog
It's jealous of lines.

The beautiful line is broken
By other line
They make a curve line.
Who has seen this curve line?

Because of jealous
On the beauty of other lines
No line can remain as it is.

-When a line is broken
  It becomes a curve line-

Translated by Jin, Cheol-Bo

# 마음의 고향

가자!
마음의 고향으로
바람에 보리 싹과 콩잎이
드러누운 벌판을 떠나

마음은
텅 빈 소라의 껍질
바다가 그리워지면
밀물에 담그었다

수평선
멀리 머얼리 밀려 갈 때
덩달아
텅 빈 미음으로

소라의 껍질에
희망을 가득 담고
머어언
바다로 향하여

외로이 떠돌다
저 멀리 머얼리
가자!
마음의 고향으로…

# Home of my heart

Let's go!
To my home of heart
After passing a field
Of barley sprouts and bean leaves are laid

My heart is
An empty conch shell
When I miss the sea
I dip it in flood tide

When water goes away
Far to the horizon
My emptied heart follows
The water at low tide.

Fill the conch shell
With hope
I go
To the sea in far

After wondering alone
Let's go
Far and far
Toward my home of heart...

Translated by Jin, Cheol-Bo

# 시인이여!

바람에
설령, 태풍이 불지라도
꺼지지 않는 촛불이여!

이상은 하나의 현실을
침체된 욕망의 씨앗은
고독을 잉태하는 조각이여!

용서할 수도
받지도 못할 마음으로
스산히 멀어져 가는 구름

못 만날 줄 알면서도
여인의 가르매 길로 걷는
개미의 걸음

짧은 시간의
니코틴과 알콜은 정신을
몽롱하게 만든 건널목

당신의 자태에
지나가는 나그넨
웃음을 파는 꽃이었소

# Poet!

Neither Wind
Nor even typhoon
Cannot blow out the candle!

Ideal bears reality
A seed of depressed desire
Is a piece bearing loneliness

Neither mind of forgiveness
Nor unforgiveness
The cloud slides away slowly

Knowing that I cannot meet her
I walk slowly along the narrow road
Like an ant

In a short while
Nicotine and alcohol cross me
And make me drunk

Your feature
Gives smile
To the way farer.

녹슬은 언어는
바람 일지 않는 곳에서
나부끼고

내 마음 속
동그라미 그리던 학도
이젠, 수직으로 높이 솟아날아라

My rusted words
Flutter in the place
Where no wind arise

Crane,
Stops draw circles in me,
And fly up high vertically into air.


Translated by Jin, Cheol-Bo

# 삶 · 2

연륜 속에 오가며
발자국으로 이루어진 길

과거에 사는 것이 아니라
미래에 그리고 현재에 사는 것

살리려는 불은 꺼지고
끌려는 불은 살아나는 것

한 장의 종이로 변해 가는 학은
벽에 걸린 수건이고 싶다

# Life · 2

While piling experiences
A way made of footpath

We don't live in the past
We live in future and present

The fire we try to make goes out
The fire we try to go out rises up.

A crane being changed into a piece of paper
Wants to be a towel hanging on the wall.

Translated by Jin, Cheol-Bo

# 분수(噴水)

누르면

누를수록

하늘 높이 치솟는

외로움

# Water fountain

The more being pressed

The higher soared skyward

And meets loneliness

Translated by Jin, Cheol-Bo

# 아가 송(頌)

아가야!
넌, 엄마가 아빠보다
더 사랑하거든
엄마를 닮아라!

아가야!
넌, 아빠가 엄마보다
더 사랑하거든
아빠를 닮아라!

아가야!
엄마와 아빠보다도
더 사랑해 주는 분이 있으면
넌, 그 사람을 닮아라!

# Praising a baby

Baby!
If your mom loves you
More than your dad
You will take after your mom

Baby!
If your dad loves you
More than your mom
You will take after your dad

Baby!
If someone loves you
More than your mom and dad
You will take after that person.

Translated by Jin, Cheol-Bo

# 부채

내가
너를 좋아함은
네가 좋아서가 아니라
네 바람이오

내가
너를 좋아함은
네가 좋아서가 아니라
네 젊음이오

내가
너를 좋아함은
네가 좋아서가 아니라
네 멋이오

내가
너를 좋아함은
네가 좋아서가 아니라
네 낭만이오

# Fan

Why
I like you is
Not because of you
But because of wind

Why
I like you is
Not because of you
But because of your youth

Why
I like you is
Not because of you
But because of your smartness

Why
I like you is
Not because of you
But because of your romanticism

Translated by Jin, Cheol-Bo

# 고향

날,
잊으셨습니까?
떨어져 갈 낙엽을

날,
생각하십니까?
떨어져 간 낙엽을

어쩌면
너 일런지도 모를
나를

잃어버리므로
찾을 수 있다면

날,
잊으셨습니까?
떨어져 간 낙엽을

날,
생각하십니까?
떨어져 갈 낙엽을

# Hometown

You
Forgot me?
A dead leaf falling away

You
Think of me?
A dead leaf fallen away

Maybe
The dead leaf
Could stay in you or me

By losing everything
If I can find you.

You
Forgot me?
The dead leaf fallen from you

You
Think of me?
The dead leaf falling from you

Translated by Jin, Cheol-Bo

# 아! 나는 공부 다 했습니다

가 다음에는 나
나 다음에는 다
다 다음에는 라
      · · · 死


1 더하기 2는 3
3 더하기 4는 7
7 더하기 8은 15
      · · · 死


A 다음에는 B
B 다음에는 C
C 다음에는 D
      . . . 以上


아! 나는 공부 다 했습니다.

# Ah, I finished studying

Ga and Na
Na and Da
Da and Ra
   .  . . Death

1 plus 2 is 3
3 plus 4 is 7
7 plus 8 is 15
   .  . . Death

A and B
B and C
C and D
   .  . . That's it.

Ah, I finished study

Translated by Jin, Cheol-Bo

# 가을의 단상

### 1.

청소부의 비질 소리에
외로움이 낙엽에 서리고

기다리며 사는 사람들의
붕괴된 대화만이
바람에 몸부림치며

태양의 마지막 줄긴
처마에 잠들고
대자연은 꿈을 꾸며

별빛은 가슴에 잠들고
미지 세계의 눈동잔
보석보다 더 짙다

# Stray thought of fall

1.

By sound of cleaner's broom sweeping
Loneliness smears into a dead leaf

Frustrated talks
Of waiting people
Flounder in wind

When the last beam of sun light
Dozes at eave
Mother of nature falls in dreams

Star lights sleep in my hearts
Eyes toward unknown future
Shine brighter than jewels

2.

어둠에 빗줄긴 장송곡
외로움이 자화상에 서리고

가로수를 우산삼아
허공에 걸린
등을 길잡이 삼아

엊그제만 해도 이동건물은
시골뜨기 서울 구경하듯
무교동 뒷골목 주점에

오늘은
초라한 선술집에
막걸리 잔을 기울인다

2.

Rain streak in the dark is a dead march
Lonesome soaks into my portrait

Roadside trees my umbrellas
Road lamps in air
my road guide

Even days ago the vagabond
Travel around the drinking bars in Mugyodong
alley
Like a country boy in Seoul

Today
At a poor pub
I drink a bowl of makeolli

3.

바람이 문을 흔들 땐
외로움이 낙엽에 서리고

모나리자 미소 같은
들에 핀 코스모스와
들국화의 향기에

세월의 흐름 속으로
인간의 집들이 산위로
벚나무에 벚꽃같이 휴식하며

고궁 뜰 붉은 놀
벤치에는 낙엽이
자의식의 세계로 잠든다.

3.

When the wind shakes door
Loneliness stack on dead leaves

Mona Lisa smile-like fragrance
Of Wild cosmos
And mum flowers

By time goes by
People's houses moved up to hills
And nest like blossoms on cherry trees

In an old palace yard colored by red twilight
An autumn leaf on a bench
Is lost in deep thought.

Translated by Jin, Cheol-Bo

시화전 끝내고 혜화동 집 등나무
「가을의 단상」 작품 앞에서

# 제2시집 『고독한 날개』중에서
# Collection of Poems Ⅱ, 『Lonely wings』

문학풍경 詩特選

# 고독한 날개

정삼일 제 2 시집

문학풍경

# 詩人 2

속이 비었을 땐
왼쪽으로 눕고
속이 차 있을 땐
오른쪽으로 눕지요

옛날에도
현재에도
영혼은
오른쪽으로 기우는데

빛바랜
책표지 모양
왼쪽으로만
자꾸 눕는 육신

詩나
쓰다가
죽어서나
바로 눕지요.

# Poet 2

When my inside is empty
I turn to lie on my left side
And when it is filled up
I lie on my right side

My soul prefers
The right side
Both when I was young
And, now, old;

And still my flesh
Would lie on its left side
Like an old yellowed
Book cover

I will just keep on
Writing poetry though I may
Come to lie the right way
When I am dead.

Translated by Kim, Yuhn-Bok

# 고독(孤獨)한 날개

### 1.

아무것도 남지 아니한
텅 빈 공허한 시간

세월의 흐름 속으로
무채색 멜로디는
귀밑에서 맴돌고

괴로운 육체는 밤으로
누운 영혼은 자아로

응고한 영육은
이리저리 뒹굴어도 편하지 아니한
수술대에 누운 환자올시다.

# Lonely Wings

### 1.

Nothing has left
In a moment of emptiness

Hearing a colorless melody
Through the passing of time

Like a patient on
The bed of operationAnd my painful body
Rolling into the night
The soul lying down
Into itself

And stark body and soul
Uneasy rolling this way and that

2.

아무것도 남지 아니한
텅 빈 공허한 시간

가증스러운 껍질을
벌거벗은 몸뚱이에 휘감고
자국을 남긴 사람들 …

붕괴된 대화는
그림자와 춤을 추고

승화된
수증기와 연기는
어디로 가오리까?

2.

Nothing has left
In a moment of emptiness

People with hateful skins
Covering bare bodies
Leaving traces of fucking,

And dialogues stopped
Dancing with shadows

Where are the sublimated
Steam and smoke gone ?

3.
아무것도 남지 아니한
텅 빈 공허한 시간

하얀 사랑의 깃 속에
기다림은 쓰레기통에 휘말려
곰팡이가 서렸고

바보가 되는 천재를 낳으신 것은
어머님의 최대 실수임에

피로한 영혼은
망각의 피로를 잃은 채
외진 비탈길에서 저문다.

3.

Nothing has left
In a moment of emptiness

In the white breast of love
Waiting becomes the dust bin
Of must

And the worst mistake of mother
Was to give a birth to a fool
Who could be a genius at
The same moment

And a tired soul
Ends up in a lonely road
Forgetting everything.


Translated by Kim, Yuhn-Bok

# 월류봉(月留峰)

山보다도
높이

물보다도
깊이

떠 있는
보름달 사이로

여인(麗人)의
자태(姿態)인 듯

우뚝 솟은
나그네.


註 : 월류봉(충북 영동군 황간면에 있는 산)

# Wollyubong

Higher
Than mountains

Deeper
Than water

Beside
Floating full moon

In a shape of
Beautiful lady

A traveller
stands tall


Note: Wollyubong (Mountain in Hwangganmyeon Yeongdongun
Cheongbuk)

Translated by Jin, Cheol-Bo

# 채석장을 바라보며

삼막사
가는 길목에

山을
옷을 벗기고
가죽을 벗기면서

웃으면서 출근한 길
웃으면서 퇴근하잔다.

山을
천 갈래 만 갈래로
갈기갈기

TNT로 터트리면서
안전 제일이란다.

山바위를
분쇄기로
가루를 만들면서

채석장은 옆으로 커지며
환경 보호하잔다.

# Looking at a stone pit

On the way to
Sammaksa Temple

People strip
And skin
The mountains

They go to work with smile
And come home with smile

Mountains
They break
Into thousands of pieces

They blow up TNTs
And say safety is best

The rocks from the mountain
With crushers
They break into powder

The stone pit grows wider sideway
But they say nature protection

山은
피를 토하며
눈물을 흘린다.


1992년 10월 3일

The mountain
Vomits blood
And sheds tears.


October 3, 1992.

Translated by Jin, Cheol-Bo

# 질(質)과 양(量)

있는 者는
밖으로
커지고

없는 者는
안으로
커진다.

그러기에

있는 者는
줄이기 위하여
질(質)이고

없는 者는
채우기 위하여
양(量)이다.

# Quality and quantity

The rich
Grow
Externally

The poor
Grow
Internally

Thus

The rich
Value quality
In order to reduce the bulks

The poor
Value the quantity
In order to refill their stomachs.

Translated by Jin, Cheol-Bo

# 가난한 농부

허기진 배를
물 한 모금 마시고
헛기침 한 번 하면
꺼질 배.

세월은
가도
외출에 부끄러운
엄지발가락.

빛바랜 책표지 모양
퇴색해 가는 농부
얻을 것은 잃고
잃을 것은 얻은 세상

가난과 친구 되어
익숙해진
구두는 넓은 혀를
내놓은 채 드러누웠다.

# The poor farmer

Drinks a cup of water
To fill up his empty stomach
But a dry cough
Empties his stomach

Long time
Has passed
But his big toe
Is shy while his master is out

Like an old book cover
The farmer is bleached
He loses things he should gain
He gets things he should avoid in this world

The shoe
Became friends with poverty
Lied down tiredly
Sticking out its wide tongue

Translated by Jin, Cheol-Bo

# 詩人은 사랑으로써 산다

큰소리 한 번만 질러도
금시 눈물 흘릴 듯 큰 눈
살짝 건드려도
터질 것 같은 봉숭아 풋물
詩人은
사랑으로써 산다.

그녀의 손은 따뜻했다
마음만큼이나
언제부터인가
나도 모르게
내 주머니 속에
호두와 대추를 넣어 놓았다.

건강하라고
건필하라고
보잘 것 없는
나를 사랑하는 마음
나에겐 줄 것이 없어
내 마음이 더 아프다.

# A poet lives with love

With my one shout
Eyes with full of tears
With a slight touch
Bursting peach cheeks
This poet
Lives with love

Her hands were warm
Like her heart
I don't know when
But I began to keep
Walnuts and jujubes in my pocket

For my health
For me to be a good writer
You pray for me, a humble man.
Because I have nothing to give you
My heart really aches me.

사랑하자
더욱더, 사랑하자
내 맘속에
모든 것을 주더라도
나보다
더 사랑하자.

I will love you
I will love you more and more
I will give you
Everything I have
I will love you
More than myself

Translated by Jin, Cheol-Bo

# 농부(農夫)

죽음이 나를 부른다
갈비뼈 사이로 고랑을 갈고
찬바람이 분다.

단식법으로
위장을 보호한다는 변명으로
굶어버리는 것이

밥 먹듯이 익숙해져 가는
위장은 이리저리 누워도
편하지 아니한 뒤틀림

몸을 지탱하기
힘들어져 가는 척추
가난한 만큼 허리가 굽는구나!

# Farmer

Death is calling me
Through furrows between the ribs.
Cold wind passes

Hungry but
I pretend a fast
To protect my stomach

As much as having meals
My stomach should be used to hunger
But twists even though I toss and turn

To support my upper body
My spine is getting weaker
My back bends forward as poor as I am

Translated by Jin, Cheol-Bo

# 병풍(屛風)

죽은 者는
병풍 뒤에 누워 있고
산 者는
병풍 앞에 누워 있다.

다만, 보이게
보이지 않게
조그마한
벽 하나

이것이
나에게
때로는
멀리

때로는
가까이
주워진
운명.

# Folding screen

A dead man
Lies behind the folding screen
A living man
Lies before the folding screen

It's simply
To be seen
Or not to be seen
By asmall wall

Sometimes
It is
Far
To me.

Sometimes
It's a closely approaching
Destiny
To me

Translated by Jin, Cheol-Bo

# 선인장

잘라 놓으면
잘라질수록

안으로
안으로 더

아픔을
안고

성장하는
그리움.

# Cactus

The more
You cut me

The more
Stronger inside

Hugging pain
In my arms

I can get energy
To grow up

Translated by Jin, Cheol-Bo

# 사랑 2

당신 앞에서는
내가 바보가 되고

내 앞에서는
당신이 바보가 되는

바보 같은
사랑을 하자.

# Love 2

Before you
I become a fool

Before me
You become a fool

Let's love
Like fools

Translated by Jin, Cheol-Bo

# 네가 되리라!

내가
품어도
내 것이 아니요

네가
품어도
네 것이 아니니

네가
내 품에 안겨
내가 되느니

내가
네 품에 안겨
네가 되리라!

# I will be you

I
Hug you
But you are not mine

You
Hug me
But I am not yours

You,
Rather than being mine
After being hugged by me

I
Will be yours
After being hugged by you

Translated by Jin, Cheol-Bo

# 비 오는 날

맑은 하늘을
먹구름이 갉아 먹고
나의 몸을 감싸주는 어둠

실없이 오는 비에
바지와 저고리 적시고

가로수를 우산 삼아
검은 허공에 걸린
등을 길잡이 삼아

어둠을 헤치며
님을 그리워하는
외로운 사람들!

바람에 나부끼는
가냘픈 여인(麗人)의
젖가슴에도

한 방울의 연속이
사뿐 사푼
수를 놓기 시작한다.

# Rainy day

The black clouds
Munch the clear sky
The darkness enfold me

Unwelcomed rain
drenched my pants and shirt

With the roadside trees as umbrellas
With the road lamp hung in black air
As guiders

The lonely people
Who miss their lovers
Wonder around In darkness

On the bosom
Of a charming lady
Flagging in wind

The falling water drops
Begin
To embroider

Translated by Jin, Cheol-Bo

# 사(死)

生 〉 死
나는 외로웠다.

生 = 死
나는 외로웠다.

生 〈 死
나는 외로웠다.

어쩌면 바보스러운
네가 더 좋았다.

# Death

Life 〉 death
I was lonely

Life = death
I was lonely

Life 〈 death
I was lonely

I wish I were a fool
Like you

Translated by Jin, Cheol-Bo

# 산(山)

山은
목욕하고 나면
소녀(少女)가 된다.

山은
목욕하고 나면
화가(畵家)가 된다.

山은
목욕하고 나면
정교(情交)한 여인(麗人)이 된다.

山은
목욕하고 나면
어머니가 된다.

# Mountain

Mountain
Becomes a girl
After taking a bath

Mountain
Becomes a painter
After taking a bath

Mountain
Becomes a beautiful sexy woman
After taking a bath

Mountain
Becomes a mother
After taking a bath

Translated by Jin, Cheol-Bo

1971년 0시문학 시화전 중
국립문화원 전시관 앞에서 동인들과 함께

제3시집

『혼자라는 것이 외로운 건 아니다』중에서

Collection of Poems Ⅲ,

『Single is not lonely』

# 혼자라는 것이 외로운 건 아니다

바람이 불어 좋은 날은
바람이 불어야 한다
라일락 향기
담 넘겨주듯
바람을 안고 산다
바람을 안고 잔다

바람이
아플 때
그리워지는 건
높은 산
넓은 바다
사람이다

바람은
혼자라는 것이
외로운 건 아니다
아무도
없다는 게
더 외롭다

# Single is not Lonely

I accept and enjoy the wind
Flying up to me over the fence;
I also want to share the lilac
Fragrance of mine with those
Over the fence
On a sweet windy day;

My wind always longs for
The lofty hill, the vast sea
And people
When it feels worn out
Or sick;

My wind feel lonely
Not when it is alone
But when there's no one
To accept it;

이런 날은 왠지
제 그림자에게
부끄럽지 않게
어디론가
멀리 머얼리
날아가고 싶다.

And on such a day
It wants to fly far,
Far, away
To feel unashamed
Of its own shadow.

Translated by Kim, Yuhn-Bok

# 꽃

이 세상에서
가장 아름다운 꽃은
당신의 마음에 꽃이요

꽃이긴 꽃이되
향기가 없음은
죽음의 꽃이요

향기가 있되
지조가 없는 것은
버려진 꽃이요

지조가 있되
낭만이 없음은
잊어버린 꽃이요.

# Flower

The best flower
In the world
Is a flower in your heart

But a flower
With no fragrance
Is a flower of death

And a flower with fragrance
Yet with no constancy
Is a flower to be thrown away

And a flower with constance
Yet with no romance
Is a flower to be forgotten

Translated by Kim, Yuhn-Bok

# 산

산에
산에 사는
새는

산이
좋아
산에 산다네

오르면
오를수록
고개를 숙이게 하고

내려가면
내려갈수록
고개를 든다

여명은
흑백이지만
황혼은 컬러이다.

# Mountain

In mountains
Living in mountains
The birds

Mountains
They like mountains
So they live there

Climbing higher
Your neck
Drop down deeper

Descending lower
Your neck
Rises up

The dawn
Is black and white
But twilight is colorful.

Translated by Jin, Cheol-Bo

# 탑(塔)

생사고락
행복과 불행의 연속
벗어남으로 고독은 끝나고
개척뿐인 일만 남았다

모든 것을 버림으로
얻을 수 있다는 지혜만이
어두우면 어두울수록
빛이 나는 별

올바로
하루를 살더라도 정의롭게
언제라도 대의명분이 있다면
죽을 각오로

조그마한 풀잎에도
정과 애착을 갖고
여명은 흑백, 황혼은 컬러로
묵묵히 솟는 여정.

# Tower

Life, Death, Suffering and Pleasure
After repeating those happiness and unhappiness
My loneliness is over
Only exploration is ahead of me

Gaining by losing all
That wisdom is
A star shining brightly
In the dark.

For justice
I live even a day
For justice
I will fight with my life

I will love and be sympathy
Toward even a small leaf
Since dawn is black and white, twilight is colorful
I will go along the road in silence

Translated by Jin, Cheol-Bo

# 병원에서

은행나무에
나뭇잎만큼
노란 환자들이
많다

바람이 분다
공중전화에서
詩 아닌
小說을 쓰고 있다.

# At a hospital

There are many
Yellow patients
As many
As leaves on a ginko tree

Wind blows
In a public phone booth
I write a novel
Not a poem

Translated by Jin, Cheol-Bo

# 사랑 〈 잊기 = 아픔

당신을 사랑하기에는
2배가 아팠습니다

당신이 아플 때는
2×3인 6배가 아팠습니다

당신을 잊기 위해서는
3×6인 18배가 아팠습니다

사랑하기보다도
잊기가 더 어려운 아픔.

# Love ⟨forgetting = pain

It hurt me 2 times
To love you

It hurt me 6 times by 2 x 3
When you were sick

It hurt me 18 times by 3 x 6
To forget you

Rather than loving you
Forgetting hurts me more

Translated by Jin, Cheol-Bo

# 당신을 생각할 때, 나는 외로워진다.

당신은 나를 볼 수 없지만
나는 당신을 볼 수 있었노라
보고프니까

당신은 나의 소리를 들을 수가 없지만
나는 당신의 소리를 들을 수가 있었노라
그리우니까

당신은 나를 생각할 수 없지만
나는 당신을 생각할 수 있었노라
행복하니까

당신은 나를 말할 수 없지만
나는 당신을 말할 수 있었노라
사랑하니까

# Whenever I think of you, I am lonely

You could not see me
But I could.
Because I missed you

You could not listen to me
But I could
Because I longed for you.

You could not think of me
But I could
Because I am happy

You could not talk about me
But I could
Because I love you


Translated by Jin, Cheol-Bo

# 그림자

당신을 위하여
존재하는지
날, 위해서
존재하는지

내가 서 있으면
당신은 눕지만
내가 누우면
당신은 사라집니다

정든 사람
헤어질 때
멀리서 뒤돌아
손 흔들 듯

내가
서 있으므로
당신이 안식이 된다면
기꺼이 서 있겠습니다.

# Shadow

Wonder
Whether I exist for you
Or
You exist for me

While I stand
You lie down
While I lie down
You disappear

As we wave
For farewell
Until our dear person
Goes far away

If you feel
Comfortable
By my standing
I will be willingly standing for you.

Translated by Jin, Cheol-Bo

# 아카시아

이산 저산 다 잡아먹은 아궁이
전쟁과 가난, 굶주림
붉게 물든 헐벗은 山河
조금만 비가 와도 홍수가 지고
조금만 가물어도 거북이 등같이
갈라지는 땅

고사리손으로 씨를 모아
누런 봉투에 담아 공중살포 하던 시절
씨로, 뿌리로 왕성한 번식
산과 제방을
씨줄과 날줄로 얽매어
수해 방지에 세운 공

짙은 향기에 물들인 향수
허기짐에 먹고 또 먹어도
배를 채울 수 없는 꽃
독사가 파수꾼 되어
산을 오르지 못하던 추억
이제는 제거하기에 바쁜 너

# Acacia

Kitchen furnaces ate all mountains
War, poverty, hunger
Devastated red hills and streams
Flooded land by a little amount of raining,
By no rain for a while
Dried and cracked land like turtle back

Once the fern-like-hands
Collected seeds in the envelops
And tossed in the air to spread widely
The seeds and the roots propagated
On mountains and banks
As latitudes and longitudes
A great deed for preventing the flood.

The strong fragrance was nostalgia
I ate and ate hungerly
But the flowers could not fill my emptied stomach
In my memory the poisonous snakes
Kept me away as guards
From the mountains
Now we busily cut you down

나무를 때던 대신
석탄과 십구공탄 대체로
많은 인명을 빼앗아 갔지만
붉은 山河를 푸르게 만든 공
독사와 네가 사라져 가는
시간의 흐름 속으로 역사가 말한다.

Instead of woods
Coal and yuntan took the place
Even many people's lives were taken
The green mountains and blue rivers are their deed.
History tells the poisonous snakes and you
Fade out in time flow

Translated by Jin, Cheol-Bo

# 부부(夫婦)

남편은 의처증

아내는 의부증

둘이 떨어져서는

살 수 없는 삶.

# Husband and wife

Husband has delusional jealousy of wife
Wife has delusional jealousy of husband
However,
They can not live separated from each other.

Translated by Jin, Cheol-Bo

# 비 오는 바다

더러운 분진을 안고 내려와
이 땅에 묻어두고
정화되어

빗방울은
영원한 승자가 없는
왕관을 쓰고

나, 언젠가는
고향으로 돌아가리라고
타이프를 치며

초생달에다
보름달처럼
별들을 주워 담는다

# Sea in the rain

Comes down hugging with dirty dust
Bury it underground
To purify

All rain drops
Wear crowns
But cannot be winners for good.

It types as
I, someday,
Will go back to my home.

I collect and put the starts
In a crescent moon
Until it becomes a full moon

Translated by Jin, Cheol-Bo

# 은사(恩師)

지금은 가로수가 감나무인
충북 영동 내 고향
서울로 공부하러 갔다가

방학 때, 고향을 찾아와
감나무 밑에 서있었다
뒤에서 누군가 두 눈을 가린다

한참 운동하고 활발한 나이
어떤 놈이야! 하고
소리를 지를 수 있는 상황

무심코 손을 더듬어 보니
어느 분이 시계를 차셨군요! 하고
돌아서 보니

이제는 정년퇴직이 얼마 안 남은
중학교 때 호랑이
체육 선생님

가시고 난 뒤
가만히 생각을 해보니
아찔하다

# My Grateful Teacher

My hometown Yeongdong Chungbuk has
The persimmon trees as the street trees
I left for Seoul to study

In vacation, I came home
While I stood under a persimmon tree
Someone blocked my eyes behind me.

As a muscled and vigorous young man
I could shout out
"Who the hell are you!"

I fumbled the hand and said
"Oh, you wear a watch"
I turned around to see the person

He was my middle school P.E. teacher
Who with a nickname of Tiger.
His retirement was near.

After he was gone
I knew I had
A critical moment

욕을 했더라면
나를 보고
배은망덕한 제자라고…

앞으로 모든 말과 행동을 조심하라고
실제로 산교육을 가르쳐주신
선생님

오십이 넘은 나이에도
감나무를 보면 떠오르는
고향과 선생님.

If I cursed him
I would be
An ungrateful former student to him.

He gave me a live lesson
To watch my words and behaviors
All the time

Even in my age of 50s
Whenever I see a persimmon tree
I remember my hometown and that teacher.

Translated by Jin, Cheol-Bo

# 추풍령

높은 山
아침에 안개가 자욱하면
낮에는 포근함에
세수시키고 떠나는 곳

구름이 춤을 추면
안개가 없듯이
샤워시키고
잠시 머물다 가는 곳

서리가 내리면
추움에
하이얀 짐을
내려놓고 가는

인지자(仁智者)의 山
물이
동쪽으로 흐르면 낙동강
서쪽으로 흐르면 금강

# Hill Chupungryeong

The morning fog
Hugs the lofty mountain
Comfortably in day time
And leaves after washing its face.

Dancing clouds
After fog goes away
Give a shower for a while
And leave away

The frost bite
In cold air
Unloads the white luggage
And leaves

The generous and wise mountain.
The water
Going to east is River Nakdonggang
And going to west is River Geumgang

Translated by Jin, Cheol-Bo

# 실향민(失鄉民)

가고 싶어도
가지 못하는
고향산천
가야만 한다
만나야만 한다
기다림이 어느덧 반세기

할아버지, 할머니
아버지, 어머니
부부
형제
며느리
손자

장독대 위에
된장, 고추장
간장
건제순으로
잘 정리된
하나의 가족사진

# Displace person

I want to go
But I can't go
To my hometown
I have to go
I have to meet them
I waited for a half decade.

Grandfather, grandmother,
Father, mother,
Husband and wife
Brothers
Daughter-in-law
Grand children


On the pot platform
The pots of dwenjang, gochujang
And ganjang
Arranged along
With drying order
Is a nice family picture

밤하늘에
선명하게 보이던
많은 별들
지척에 두고도
가지 못하는
그리운 고향

The countless starts
Shining clearly in the night sky
My hometown
Even thought is near me
But I can't go
While missing it.

Translated by Jin, Cheol-Bo

# 말하라! 그 날의 진실을

## - 노근리 양민학살 사건 -

평화를 뜻하던 비둘기가
어느 날 갑자기 쌍굴다리에서
빨간 고무장갑을 벗고
독수리로 변하였네

가난과 약자의 아픔이었기에
눈을 가지고도, 귀가 있어도
입이 있어도 말하지 못했던
양민학살

노근리 사람들은 두 번 죽었는지도 모른다
미군은 인민군이 두려워 그들을 죽였고
우리는 미국이 두려워
그들의 진실을 외면했다

서기만 하면 죽는 겨
나오기만 하면 죽는 겨
삶은
죽음보다도 더 처절했다

# Tell! The truth of the day
## -Massacring civilians at Nogunri-

A pigeon symbolizing peace
One day, suddenly, in the doubled tunnel bridge
Took off its red gloves
And changed into an eagle

Because they were poor and had the pain the
weak
Even though they had eyes, ears and mouths
But could not tell the truth
That it was a massacring civilians.

Perhaps people of Nogunri died twice
American soldiers killed them in fear of North
Korean armies.
We were afraid of US Army
So we faced away from the truth.

One who stood was killed
One who came out was killed, too.
Life
Was more miserable than death.

반세기가 흘러도 쌍굴다리가
아직도 눈을 감지 못하고
두 눈을 크게 뜨고 있다
그날의 진실을 밝혀달라고 …

A half century has passed, but the double tunnel
Still could not close eyes
Opens its eyes widely
Demanding us to uncover the truth.

Translated by Jin, Cheol-Bo

경상남북도, 부산, 대구교도소 16곳 순회공연 시낭송

# 제4시집 『황금동 연가』중에서
# Collection of Poems IV,
# 『Love Poems of Hwanggeumdong』

정삼일 제4시집

# 황금동 연가

나는 산에만 가면 부자이다
지천에 깔린 누런 지폐 치우기에 바쁘다
나무는 은행인가 보다
남아도 매년 발행하는 것을 보면

# 황금동 연가

까치 한 마리
늦노을 끄트머리
낙엽을 긁는구나

곱고 단정하게 빗은
선명한 가슴
하얀 마음

너 같은 색시
하나 있었으면
좋겠어.

# Love Poems of Hwanggeumdong

A magpie
At the end of late twilight
Scratches the dead leaves

Neatly combed
Clear chest
And its white mind

Wish I had
A woman
Like you

Translated by Jin, Cheol-Bo

# 목향인(木向人)

모랄은
풍한서습(風寒署濕)에
옹이가 져도
묵묵히 말이 없다

주면
주는 만큼
때로는
더 많이 성장하는

더울 때는
그늘을 만들어 주고
추울 때는
홀연히 벗어 주는

사랑하고픈
여인(麗人)
배반하지 않는
나무는 거짓이 없다.

# A tree-like man

Tree
Is quiet
Even though knots are made
By cold wind and hot moisture

Grows
As much as given
Sometimes
More than being given

When it is hot
It makes shade
When it is cold
It strips off itself

Tree like my dear lady
Whom I long for
Is not treachery
But faithful

Translated by Jin, Cheol-Bo

# 대추

비온 뒤
가을 햇볕

잎보다
더 푸른 대추

불 항아리
새색시

싱그러움에
얼굴 붉힌다.

# jujube

After rain
In the fall sunlight

More than leaves
The jujube are darker green

The fire pot
The new bride

Is blushed
By its vitality

Translated by Jin, Cheol-Bo

# 그리움

바다를
보고 싶다는 이유로
여인(麗人)을
만나야만 되겠다

숲으로 가잔다
그러지요 하고
이른 새벽에
액셀러레이터를 밟는다

먼 길을
임 보러 가듯
희망을 안고
달린다

숲속에 사나이는
바다를
바다의 여인은
숲속을 그리워하며

숲속에는
그리움이 없단다
없는 것을 보기 위해
브레이크를 잡는다.

# Missing

With an excuse of
Missing the sea
I'll have to
Meet my fair lady.

She wants to go to a forest.
I say yes
And accelerate up
In early dawn

As if I go far
To see my dear lady
I drive
With armful hope

The man in the forest
Misses the sea
The woman in the sea
Misses the forest

Someone said nothing to miss
In the forest
But I take a break
To see the nothing.

Translated by Jin, Cheol-Bo

# 그리움 2.

풀 베고
돌아서면

숨바꼭질하듯
고만큼

또,
자라 있네.

# Missing 2.

As soon as I turn around
After cutting grass

As if we are playing
The hide-and-seek game

Again
They grew up

Translated by Jin, Cheol-Bo

# 욕실에서

바다이다
파도가 치지 않는

강이다
흐르지 않는

시냇물이다
고기가 살지 않는

눈을 감으면
파도가 치고

강이 흐르고
고기가 사는

# In the bathroom

Its a sea
But no waves crash

Its a river
But no water flows

Its a stream
But no fishes live

If I close my eyes
The waves are hitting

The river flows
The fishes are living.

Translated by Jin, Cheol-Bo

# 독도

가라앉는 땅은
숫아오르는 땅을
그리워한다

포크레인 가지고
파헤쳐도
얼마 안 되는 섬

숫한 세파(世波)에도
숫한 세월에도
흔들리지 않는 섬

조상이 물려주고
후손이 살아가야 할 터전
잃을 수는 없다

모든 사람
어린아이도 아는 것을
억지 쓰고 싶은 심정

하와이 진주만 침략전쟁
가미가제 떨어졌다고
일본 땅인가.

# Dokdo

The sinking land
Envies
The rising land

So small
Even an excavator can demolish

By numerous raging waves
By countless years
The island has never be shaken

Our ancestors handed down
Our descendant will live on
No way we will lose the place

Everybody knows
Even little kids know
But you insist

Is Pearl Harbor of Hawaii yours
Because Japanese kamikaze planes crashed into
the ground
While the war of attacking on pearl harbor?

Translated by Jin, Cheol-Bo

# 둘이서 하나가 되어

한 사람은
다리가 없고
또 한사람은
팔이 없다

다리가 없는 사람은
다리를
팔이 없는 사람은
팔을 더 좋아했다

없는 것을
서로가 서로를 보살핌 속에
있는 것보다
없는 것을 더 사랑하며

둘이서
하나가 되어
누구보다도 더
행복한 삶.

# The two become one

One has
No legs
Other has
No arms

The legless man
liked legs more than arms.
The armless man
liked arms more than legs

In order to cover
Deficiencies of each other
They love more the part
They don't have

The two became
One
The happier life
Than any others

Translated by Jin, Cheol-Bo

# 환경오염도

숫하게 스쳐 지나가는
죽음들이
아무 말 없이
바람을 몰고 간다

물보다
사람이 더 많고
깨끗한 물보다
더럽혀진 물이 더 많다

하루를 천재로 살면
이틀이 불편하지만
하루를 바보처럼 살면
하루는 편안하기에

오염된 바다를
정화하기 위해서
태풍도
몸살을 앓고 있다.

# Level of environmental pollution

Numerous
Passing deaths
Drives the wind
In silence

Than water
More people
Than clean water
More contaminated water

If you live a day as a genius
You'll have two uncomfortable days
If you live a day as a fool
You'll have one comfortable day

To purify
The polluted seas
Typhoons
Are exhausted

Translated by Jin, Cheol-Bo

# 사랑하는 것은

사랑하는 것만큼
쉬운 것이 없다

사랑하는 것만큼
어려운 게 없다

쉬운 것과 어려운 것
백지 한 장

사랑하는 것은
당신의 마음.

# Love is

Nothing is easier
Than love

Nothing is more difficult
than love

Easy and difficult things are
Front and back side of paper

Love is
In your heart

Translated by Jin, Cheol-Bo

# 수성 못 2.

여명에
검은 이불
섬 속에 개어놓고
일출을 맞는 새색시

낮이면
하얀 캔버스 수채화 그리다
잔잔한 바람에도
깜빡깜빡

붉게 타는 저녁놀
일몰에 돌아 온 농부
냉가슴 풀어
맞이하는 새색시

밤이면
하얀 이불
색색이 수놓은 불빛
별 따다 잠든다.

# Soo-Seung Pond 2.

In dawn
It folds up its quilt of darkness
And puts it on cornered islands,
To be ready to meet the sun rise;

In day it draws
A water-color painting
On the white canvas with lights
Glittering softly in the wind

And under the burning
Sun set clouds, becomes a bride
Receiving its cold-hearted farmer
Into its warm heart;

At night
Sleeps under the white bedding
Embroidered with colorful lights
In dream of gaining a star.

Translated by Kim, Yuhn-Bok

# 낙엽

나는
산에만 가면
부자이다

지천에 깔린
누런 지폐
치우기에 바쁘다

나무는 은행인가 보다
남아도
매년 발행하는 것을 보면

# Dead leaf

I
am rich
In a mountain

The countless
Golden paper money
I am busy with sweep away

Trees must be banks
Even already excessive
They produce money every year

Translated by Jin, Cheol-Bo

# 뻥튀기 집

오일장서는
시골장터
뻥튀기 집

아낙네 · 할머니 손에
쌀, 보리, 옥수수 …
보따리 풀어놓고

삶, 희망
세상사 이야기
뻥튀기며

열다섯에 시작하여
아직까지 한다는
주름살 검게 그을린 할아버지

뻥 소리에 놀라
귀 막는
아이들과 노인들

주인 따라 나오는 누렁이
뻥 소리에도 구수한 냄새 맡으며
자장가인 듯 졸고 있다.

# Popcorn House

A popcorn house
In the fifth day market
In a country

Sags of rice, barley, corn...
Carried by wives and grandmas
Are spreaded

Life, hope
And mundane matters
Are popped up too

From fifteen till now
I do this job
Said the dark winkled old man

By the blasting sound of popcorn machine
Block their ears
Children and old folks

Popcorn man's yellow dog
Falls asleep
With the noise and smell as a lullaby

Translated by Jin, Cheol-Bo

# 인생(人生)

살아생전
조그마한 항아리 속으로
못 들어가고

죽어서는
조그마한 항아리
채우지 못하네.

# Life

It's
a small can't go
into the jar

And died is not
fill a small
jar one's lifetime.

Translated by Jin, Cheol-Bo

# 문인들

옛날에는
체육인 · 문인들
다 미련하고
바보라 했다

그러나
현재
체육인도
돈방석에 앉았다

언젠가는
문인들도
돈방석에 앉을 날
올 것이다

병원에
육체를 치유하는 의사와
정신을 치유하는 문인이 있어야
허가가 나는 세상.

# Writers

In old days
Sportsmen and writers
Were called
Silly and foolish

However
Today
The sportsmen
Sit on money cushions.

Some day
You'll see
The writers
Sit on money cushions

A hospital
Will be approved
After having physicians for body
And writers for mental care.

Translated by Jin, Cheol-Bo

# 감잎 단풍에 담은 연서

붉게 타는 저녁놀
끄트머리
갈 길은 먼데
떠날 줄 모르고

열어주지 않으면
열리지 않는
자물쇠와
열쇠

아직도
단풍은 안 들었는데
마음만 먼저 가서
물들어 있네.

# Love Letteron the Reddened Persimmon Leaf

Love burns like
The evening sun-set beauty,
Hangs on the tree
Forgetting its destiny

Like a couple of
Lock and key
Helpless until
The key opens the lock,

Though it is not
The season to turn red
My heart reaches there
Already to turn red.

Translated by Kim, Yuhn-Bok

# 산 넘고 물 건너

할머니가
산속에 길로
지팡이 짚고
올라가고 있다
언제 다 올라갈려나

할머니가
외나무다리에
지팡이 짚고
걷고 있다
언제 다 건너갈려나

곱게 차려입은 옷보다
더 예쁜 새색시
세월 앞에서는
고개 숙인
한숨 쉬는 소리.

# Across the hill across the river

An old woman
Climbs up an uphill road
On a stick
When will she reach the top ?

An old woman
Walks up one wood bridge
Across the brook, on a stick;
When will she cross the brook ?

A beautiful lady dressed up
Once she was !
Now, in front of hill of time
A deep sigh of life.

Translated by Kim, Yuhn-Bok

# 첫 사랑

초등학교 1학년
소풍 갔을 때

숨바꼭질하다가
숨을 곳을 찾던 중

숨을 곳이 없어서
치마 속으로 숨었더니

놀라움 접어두고
치마 펼쳐

감싸주던
처녀 선생님.

# First Love

It was a picnic day
When I was elementary first grader


While I was looking for a hiding place
During the hide and seek game

I had no where to hide
So I ran into the skirt of my teacher

Though she was embarrassed
Covered me up with her skirt

She hid me
The young lady teacher of me.

Translated by Jin, Cheol-Bo

시낭송에 대하여

# 제5시집 『행복을 위하여』중에서
# Collection of Poems Ⅴ,
# 『For the Sake of Happiness』

한글기획 21C 시정선 17

정삼일 제5시집

## 행복을 위하여

내가 있기에 당신이 있고
당신이 있기에 내가 있다
이름은 존재이며 다른 사람이
불러주는 것이다

도서출판
한글 BOOK

# 행복을 위하여

행복하다고 생각하는 사람만큼
행복한 사람 없고
불행하다고 생각하는 사람만큼
불행한 사람 없다

있다고 행복한 것도 아니요
없다고 불행한 法은 없는 法
모든 것 행복과 불행이
마음속에 있나니

모든 사람에게는
하나의 장점과 단점을 주었거늘
자만할 일도 없고
자학할 일도 없는 法

人間苦中
베풀고, 사랑하고
깨달음만큼
큰 행복은 없다.

# For the Sake of Happiness

No man is happier than those who
Think they are happy themselves;
No man is more miserable than those
Who think their lives are miserable.

The haves are not always happy
And the have-nots not always unhappy
And this means happiness and unhappiness
Are always made up in one's mind.

Each man is given his own merit and
Demerit; so there is no excuse for any
One to be too proud or to torture
Himself too much;

Thus the best treasure
In the painful sea of life
Is to give, to love,
No more big happiness

Translated by Kim, Yuhn-Bok

# 일곱 번 죽어

배추가
밭에서 뽑힐 때
한 번 죽고

배를 가르면서
또 한 번 죽고
소금에 절여져 또다시 죽고

모든 양념에
버무려지어 또 죽고
김장독 묻을 때 죽고

숙성 후
도마 위에서
칼에 잘리면서 또 죽고

입안에서
씹혀 또 죽어야
비로소 김치 맛을 낸다.

# After Seventh Death of a Cabbage

A cabbage dies once
When it is rooted out from the field
And when it is divided into two

By a knife, a second death;
And pickled in salt, a third death

And seasoned again by all
The other spices, fourth death
And buried down under soil, fifth death

And cut into pieces again on the chopping board
After it is dug out from under the soil, sixth
death
And it is chewed down inside human mouths,

 So, in its seventh death, it becomes a kimchi
 With its real taste.

Translated by Kim, Yuhn-Bok

# 동백꽃

입술 사이에 물린
불 속의 연기가
내 마음속에 들어왔다가

연한 연기를 내 뿜으며
바람처럼 사라지고
재만 남았습니다

그리고는
아무 말이 없었습니다
흔적도 없이

네가 있다가
빠져나간
공간의 체온

# Camellia Flower

Smoke with fire
Burning between my lips
Spreaded into my heart.

It emitted from me
And gone with wind as thin smoke
Leaving ash in me

And then
It left neither word
Nor trace

From the room it has been
I feel
Only its warmth

Translate by Jin, Cheol-Bo

# 갈대

갈 때까지
가보자 해서
갈대인가

억센 바람에
시달려 깃털 같아
억새인가

우리가
갈대라고 생각한 것은
억새이고

억새라고
생각한 것은
갈대이다

# Reed

Is it reed
Because
It runs far to the end?

Is it silver grass
Because it's a feather
Stands against the growling wind?

The reed
we've thought
is silver grass

The silver grass
we've thought
is reed

Translated by Jin, Cheol-Bo

# 만남

넌,
나를
만나기 위하여
잠시 생각하지만

난,
너를
만나기 위하여
하루 종일 생각한다

넌, 내가
인생의 일부이지만
난, 네가
인생의 전부이다.

# Meeting

You
Miss me for a moment
And meet me.

I
Miss you all day
And meet you.

To you
I am a part of your life.
To me
You are all of my life.

Translated by Jin, Cheol-Bo

# 詩와 낭송의 향기

詩가 꽃이라면 낭송은 향기요
詩가 작사라면 낭송은 노래요
詩는 읽는 사람에 따라 느낌이 다르듯이
누가 낭송하느냐에 따라
가슴에 와서 닿는 느낌이 다르다

이제는 덤으로 사는 나이에
시낭송 하다 보니
무엇이든지
뜻을 이루려면 미쳐야 하고
역시 노력 없이는 안 되는 것

먼저 암송을 하려면
백번 이상을 읽어야 하고
내용과 뜻 이해를 하면
머릿속에는 그려지는
한 폭의 그림

# Poem and Fragrance of Reciting

If a poem is a flower, reciting is fragrance
If a poem is a songwriting, reciting is a song
Different taste, different reciter
Depends on reciter
Different feelings touch each heart.

At my age of extra life
The poem reciting teaches me
Be frantic and do best
To achieve whatever you planned

Before reciting
Read more than hundred times
To understand the poem
So that I will have
A picture of it in my heart.

Translated by Jin, Cheol-Bo

# 山 일

하루를 안 가면
일주일 안간 것 같고

일주일을 안 가면
한 달 안간 것 같고

한 달을 안가면
일 년 안간 것 같아

일을 안 한다고
말하는 사람은 없지만

산일이란 무궁무진함으로
매일 가서 산에다 詩를 쓴다.

# Work on mountain

If I don't go a day
I feel like I didn't go for a week

If I don't go a week
I feel like I didn't go for a month

If I don't go a month
I feel like I didn't go for a year

No one tells
That I don't work

But the mountain wants my hand endlessly
So I go to write poems on it everyday.

Translated by Jin, Cheol-Bo

# 당신이 좋다면

당신이 좋다기에
따라 왔시유

나, 저 세상 갈 때
데려 가유

꼭,
잊지 말고유

당신이 좋다면
나, 다 따라 갈래유

# If you like

I am here
Because you like me

Take me with you
When you go to the beyond world.

For sure,
Never forget.

If you like me
I will follow you anywhere

Translated by Jin, Cheol-Bo

# 무당벌레

소름 끼치게
징그러운
애벌레

둥글게
움츠려
등 만들고

해, 달
지구
등에 지고

채소를 헤치는
진딧물의
천적.

# Ladybug

Goose-bumpy and
Creepy
A caterpillar

Stoop
Its body
To make a round back

Carries sun, moon
and earth
on its back

You're the natural enemy
To lice plants
That bother vegetables.

Translated by Jin, Cheol-Bo

# 보이지 않는 것까지

동녘 하늘 여명에
낚시바늘 하나 던져 놓고
구름 사이로
별을 낚고 있다

기분 좋은 날은
몸과 마음이 가볍고
기분 나쁜 날은
무거운 몸과 마음

내가 그를 보고 실망하듯이
누가 나를 보고 실망할까
내가 그를 좋아하듯
누가 나를 좋아하길

보이는 것과
보이지 않는 것까지
그리워하자
사랑하자

# Even invisible things

I throw a fishing needle
Into the dawn of eastern sky
Between clouds
To hook up stars

On a day I feel good
My body and mind are light
On a day I feel bad
My body and mind are heavy

As I am disappointed at him
Some one might be disappointed at me
As I like him
Hope some one likes me

Something visible
And even something invisible
I will care and
Love

Translated by Jin, Cheol-Bo

# 산에 가는 이유

하늘 아래
山과
바다와 들

山
바다와 들 끝자락
언제나 하늘

時間은
날
붙잡지 않는다

모든 괴로움
어려움 다 잊고
山에다 묻으라 한다.

# Reason why I go to a mountain

Under the sky
there are
mountains, seas and fields.

There is always sky
at the edge of
mountains, seas and fields.

Time
Does not hold
Me.

All sufferings and agonies
I will sweep away from me
And bury them in a mountain.

Translated by Jin, Cheol-Bo

# 단풍

요염한 자태로
색색이 옷을
벗어버리는 나체

혼자
보기에는
너무 아까워

가을을
흠뻑 담은
사진 한 장

내가 찍은
사진에는
내가 없다.

# Maple

A charming figure
Strips off its colorful clothes
To be nude

It's a waste
To see it
Alone

A photo
Loaded
With full of autumn

In the photo
I've taken
I'm not there

Translated by Jin, Cheol-Bo

# Cheonghak Jeong Sam-il
# (Poet and Poetry reciter)

Born in Yeongdong Chungbuk
Graduated from Seoul National University of Science and Technology
「Blood Color」 (1969), 「Zero Hour Leterature」 (1971)
「Living Place Literature」 (1997), 「Literature Colleague」 Coterie
「International Pen Korea Headquarter」 Director
「Korea Literature Association」 Ethical Committee Member, Auditor (former)
「Korea Modern Poets Association」 General Secretary (former),
Director and Ethnic Committee Chairman.
「Daegu Pen」 Auditor (former) for 12 years and Director
「Farmer Literature」 Auditor (former) Yein Literature Consultant (former)
Bi-monthly 「Cosmos Literature」 Chief Editor (2002-2012)
Buddhism Literature」 Daegu Branch Chief 「Eonjeom Poetry」 Adviser
〈Award〉
 〈Korea Number 3 Poem Reciter〉
 〈Korea Farmer Literature Award〉 , 〈Dasan Literature Grand Prize〉
 〈Georang Literature Award〉 , 〈Korean Yecho Literature Grand Prize〉
 〈Buddhism Literature Grand Prize〉 , 〈Songgang Literature-Art Grand Prize〉
 〈Maeheon Yun Bong-Gil Literature Grand Prize〉
Special Achievement Award at the 100th International Pen Foundation
Ceremony.
〈Collection of Poems〉
 『Not Even Awaking up Wind』 in 1992
 『Lonely Wings』 in 1997
 『Single is not Lonely』 in 2003
 『Love Poems of Hwanggeumdong』 in 2009
 『For the Sake of Happiness』 in 2018
〈How to Contact〉
Address : (42113) #102-401 Cheonghoro 57gil-89 Susunggu Daegu
Mobil Phone : 010-4145-3131
E-mail : samilpoet-@naver.com

시인의 마을 한·영 시선집 35

**감잎 단풍에 담은 연서**

2023년 6월 20일 1판 1쇄 인쇄
2023년 6월 25일 1판 1쇄 발행

저    자 정삼일
발행자 심혁창
마케팅 정기영
디자인 박성덕
교    열 송재덕
인    쇄 김영배
펴낸곳 도서출판 한글

우편 04116
서울특별시 마포구 신촌로 270(아현동)
수창빌딩 903호

☎ 02-363-0301 / FAX 362-8635
E-mail : simsazang@daum.net
창      업 1980. 2. 20.
이전신고 제2018-000182

* 파본은 교환해 드립니다
* 정가 15,000원
*
ISBN 97889-7073-624-2-03130